Contents

Introduction

There's No Business Like Show Business

Shakespeare wrote, "All the world's a stage" in the sixteenth century. Those words still ring true for the 2 million people who work in the American entertainment industry. These folks spend their time on stages or behind the scenes working in teams to create music, theater productions, radio broadcasts, television programs, and movies. Some have dream jobs; they are movie directors or electronic dance music disc jockeys. Others work as audio engineers, promoters, talent scouts, and other professionals who keep the wheels of the entertainment industry spinning.

Plenty of movies and TV shows focus on the business side of show business, portraying the industry as glamorous and exciting—where a creative vision always wins the day. Indeed, some entertainment jobs can be quite thrilling. But for many, even the most dazzling job involves working fifty-plus hours a week. Entertainment industry professionals often work early mornings and late nights. Many spend their days talking on the phone, giving presentations, and attending meetings, rehearsals, and promotions. About half of all people who make their careers in show business are self-employed; many of these freelancers earn less money than office workers with a steady paycheck.

The Sky Really Is the Limit

In 2014 Damian Bazadona, who runs a major entertainment marketing firm, was curious about the reality of working in the entertainment industry. This led him to conduct an anonymous survey of five hundred nonactors involved with theater, television, film, live music, and arts institutions. Bazadona found that these men and women were highly educated; 97 percent of the respondents held a bachelor's degree, and around 40 percent held graduate or advanced degrees. By way of comparison, around 32 percent of Americans held bachelor's degrees in 2014, while 12 percent had advanced degrees.

When Bazadona asked respondents to describe in one word what it was like to work in the entertainment business, the top three answers were "passion," "intensity," and "engaging." Other common descriptors were "fulfilling," "challenging," "rewarding," "meaningful," and "evolving." But such passion and intensity can take its toll. A full 46 percent of Bazadona's respondents said they had cried at work within the previous week. On the bright side, an equal number said "the sky is the limit for my career."

Brains and Talent

Anyone who wants to gain an advantage in such a highly competitive industry would do well to focus on several subjects in school. Business and math courses are very helpful in a profession sometimes referred to as the "business of show." Indeed, most decisions in Hollywood, Bollywood, New York, London, and other entertainment capitals are based on dollars and cents. Those who understand business will find themselves in demand. "People that master their financial accounting skills become extremely valuable commodities in the entertainment field," writer/producer Phil Breman told the financial website the Balance in 2016. "Those individuals that can effectively manage the budgets of all of the various television shows, digital productions and movies are like human bars of gold to most major entertainment companies."

Business and math skills are also important to those who hope to become agents, promoters, and talent scouts. These professionals deal with vendors, payrolls, royalty payments, and other money matters. Freelancers such as lighting and sound techs also need business skills to decipher complex contracts, manage money, and avoid financial pitfalls and showbiz rip-offs that are all too common.

Being familiar with technology is important to anyone hoping to get ahead in the entertainment business. Computers, software, digital

Careers in Entertainment

Occupation	Minimal Education Requirements	2015 Median Pay
Actor	Some college, no degree	$18.80 per hour
Announcer	High school diploma and training	$30,080
Art director	Bachelor's degree	$89,760
Barber, hairdresser, cosmetologist	Training program and license required	$23,710
Broadcast and sound engineer technician	Postsecondary non-degree or associate's degree	$41,780
Dancer and choreographer	Years of formal dance training	$16.85 per hour
Film and video editor and camera operator	Bachelor's degree	$55,740
Meeting, convention, and event planner	Bachelor's degree	$46,840
Music director and composer	Bachelor's degree	$49,820
Musician and singer	No formal education	$24.20 per hour
Producer and director	Bachelor's degree	$68,440
Public relations specialist	Bachelor's degree	$56,770
Writer and author	Bachelor's degree	$60,250

Source: Bureau of Labor Statistics, *Occupational Outlook Handbook*, 2015. www.bls.gov.

cameras, and other high-tech tools are central to recording, broadcasting, and film production. Getting a degree in the arts can also open doors in the entertainment industry. Producers employ graphic artists, animators, hair and makeup artists, scenery painters, interior designers, fashion and wardrobe managers, and numerous others who use their artistic talents every day on the job.

As with nearly every other industry, writing and communication skills are a big plus in show business. The industry thrives on scripts, lyrics, stories, marketing, and promotion. Most work is undertaken as part of a team, where communication and problem-solving skills are indispensable.

Finally, some necessary skills are not taught in college. "Don't forget the value of life experience," advised Breman. "For most creative positions such as a writer or director, being able to call upon certain moments in your history will also prove quite valuable. Some of the best moments in entertainment have come through the memories of their creators."

A Desire and the Fire

Whatever a person's experience or skills, it can be quite difficult to get a job in a business that attracts countless dreamers, hustlers, and true talents from every part of the globe. A successful career in the entertainment industry requires personal commitment. Showbiz wannabes need to pound the pavement, make phone calls, network continuously, and refuse to take no for an answer. As sound and lighting tech Lenny Manzo put it in his 2011 autobiography *Above the Line: A Twenty Year Career Inside the Movie Business*: "You have to have a desire for it, you also have to have a fire for it. To make it [to the top] you have to have a burning drive that borders on obsession."

A Growing Industry

The US entertainment industry is huge, and it is getting bigger every year. In 2015 entertainment and media companies generated over $630 billion and created a surge of new jobs. In Los Angeles alone, at least eight thousand new show business jobs were added in 2015. Analysts credit some of the growth to new-media outlets like Netflix, Amazon, and Hulu, which are now producing their own original shows.

The entertainment industry is expected to generate $771 billion by 2019, more than $2 trillion worldwide. That is all good news for those who want to build their careers around lights, cameras, and action. And for the tens of thousands of people who work in front of and behind the cameras and microphones, as the old song says—there's no business like show business.

Musician

What Does a Musician Do?

In 2016 Taylor Swift earned more than $170 million singing her songs to millions of fans. Country singer Garth Brooks made $70 million, while the Rolling Stones pulled in $66 million. With eye-popping numbers like these, it is easy to understand why so many singers, songwriters, and instrumentalists want to work as professional musicians. But those who dream of riding in limousines and flying to concerts in private jets should remember the old saying: A musician is someone who loads $4,000 worth of musical equipment into a $1,000 car and drives 100 miles (161 km) for a $50 engagement. For every Taylor Swift, there are thousands in that $1,000 car.

> **At a Glance**
> **Musician**
>
> **Minimum Educational Requirements**
> None, though classical musicians and opera singers need a bachelor's degree
>
> **Personal Qualities**
> Talent, dedication, good communication skills, stamina, ability to accept criticism
>
> **Working Conditions**
> Nights and weekends in bars, concert venues, and reception halls
>
> **Salary Range**
> Median pay of $24.20 an hour in 2015
>
> **Number of Jobs**
> About 173,000 in 2014
>
> **Future Job Outlook**
> Projected growth of around 3 percent by 2024

While not everyone can be the next pop superstar, many musicians use their talents to pay their bills, or at least some of them. These professional musicians play instruments and sing in front of live audiences at clubs, theaters, and other concert venues. They perform on the radio and television and record music in recording studios.

Professional musicians rely on a combination of artistic inspiration, physical skills, and business acumen. On the artistic level, good music generates a wide range of emotions. Unlike most other art forms, this provides the opportunity to forge a magical connection between the musician and the listener. While it is nearly impossible to generate creative inspiration on demand, practicing helps musicians improve their talents. Musicians practice to train their vocal cords and (depending on the instrument) the movements of their fingers, hands, arms, legs, and lips to play an instrument accurately and expertly.

Developing creative and physical skills might be difficult. But it is the business part of show business that most challenges many prospective musicians. Those who are just starting out have to act as their own agent, manager, and record producer. Musicians act as agents when they contact bars, clubs, event planners, and booking agents to book jobs, or gigs. They act as managers when they secure gigs in writing and read through contracts to ensure they are getting a fair deal. Musicians must also manage money, pay themselves and other band members, maintain equipment, and budget for transportation, food, and accommodations. Additionally, musicians must learn the art of recording so they can make audio files for promotion, sales, and social media posts. This requires developing the technical skills to handle recording equipment, computers, and music apps.

Punk rock musician Paul Diamond Blow sums up a professional musician's life on his personal blog: "If you are a musician . . . and you are trying to become successful, you will probably spend a good majority of your money, energy and free time on the band: rehearsing, writing songs, recording, booking gigs, networking, trying to get airplay, and promoting, promoting, promoting."

How Do You Become a Musician?

Education

Prospective lawyers usually take a well-traveled career path; they go to college, study law, and get a job at a law firm. However, a person who wants to become a professional guitarist, keyboardist, drummer (or other instrumentalist) does not travel such a clear-cut path. Even

A musician performs before an audience. Talent and creativity are essential for working musicians, as is knowledge of standard business practices including budgeting and promotion.

so, if someone dreams of playing their heart out in front of an adoring audience, there are numerous steps they can take to tilt the odds of success in their favor.

Some of the world's most famous musicians are self-taught; they did not go to music school, and some cannot even read music notation. Unless a person is planning to teach or perform in a symphony orchestra or opera, there are no educational requirements for becoming a musician. In this industry, there are pros and cons to obtaining a formal music education. On the negative side, some students fail to achieve desired outcomes after studying music in college. Classes focus extensively on music theory while ignoring artistic intangibles like creative inspiration. As musician Thomas Rutherford pointed out on the Careers in Music website in 2015, college music courses can actually harm some students. "Their style and individuality were stamped out by teachers pursuing proper technique," he remembered of some students. "Learning too much music theory caused them to question their musical intuition. Over time, they simply lost their love for the art."

However, Rutherford had a much more positive experience after he studied music at the University of Southern California. During his time there, he built important relationships with numerous people who shared his musical interests. Some became future bandmates and advisers. Rutherford built social networks at school that helped him make connections to important players in the music industry. He was also able to play in front of famous musicians, such as songwriter and bassist Adam Blackstone and singer Chaka Khan, at university-sponsored forums. According to Rutherford, "These otherwise inaccessible music industry giants will listen to student performances, hang around to talk after class, and will provide unique gigs and opportunities for students. Outside of a major university, opportunities like these rarely exist."

Of course, the main reason students attend music school is to improve their talents and skills. Most teachers are master musicians who pass along valuable information that might take years to learn without instruction. And knowing how to read music can open up numerous opportunities. An educated musician can teach, join an orchestra, work in theater, write scores for video games and movies, make commercials, and pick up studio gigs.

High school and college students on summer break can improve their musical knowledge by attending the numerous music camps and music programs found in nearly every state and region. Many of these programs are affiliated with colleges, universities, and conservatories.

Music camps often specialize; there are oboe camps, bassoon camps, piano camps, pipe organ camps, and camps dedicated to choral singing and opera. Camps also focus on musical styles, from jazz to classical to rock. Programs typically include private lessons, music theory, master classes, and group and solo performances. The end of the summer often features a student concert or music festival.

Some music camps, such as the Philadelphia International Music Camp & Festival, require participants to pass an audition in order to attend. Others accept students of various skill levels. Summer programs like the one at the Lamont School of Music in Denver offer college credit to precollege musicians.

Volunteer Work and Internships

Playing for little or no money is a rite of passage for musicians beginning their career—most figure that any gig is better than no gig. Musicians volunteer to play at school dances, private parties, street fairs, and other social events. These gigs help a player gain experience in front of an audience while (hopefully) building up a fan base. Musicians can use pictures and videos from nonpaying jobs to promote themselves on social media and provide demonstration recordings, or "demos," for managers and booking agents.

Musicians also volunteer to play with choirs or orchestras that perform in theatrical productions, concert halls, or performing arts centers. Many playhouses rely on volunteers to put together local productions. Some use volunteer musicians in the orchestra, while others put volunteers to work behind the scenes—setting up equipment or handing out programs. Whatever the task, volunteering for an orchestra is a great way to watch, meet, and learn from experienced musicians.

Skills and Personality

Musicians have to be very dedicated to their art. They are often required to audition and must carry on in face of rejection. Self-discipline is a necessary personality trait; musicians need to spend hours practicing to improve their technique, style, and performance abilities. Playing music almost always requires teamwork, which compels a musician to work well with other musicians, producers, directors, and conductors. Musicians need to be able to communicate clearly and accept constructive criticism gracefully. They need advertising skills to promote their performances online and in their community. And, as anyone who has ever played music professionally will agree, a musician needs stamina and physical strength. Musicians often travel extensively, keep irregular hours, transport and set up heavy sound equipment, and move around onstage for hours while holding an instrument.

On the Job

Employers

Musicians play everywhere, including sparsely populated coffeehouses, teeming subway stations, and concert halls filled with thousands of people. This makes the job experience as varied as the venues. Musicians who play pop, rock, country, or hip-hop spend many nights in clubs and bars, while jazz and classical musicians might find themselves on the concert stage.

Most nonfamous musicians are self-employed. They find full-time work and earn a living by being flexible and playing many different styles of music. They might perform with multiple rock or jazz bands so they can gig up to five times a week. They play weddings and other events, teach music to children, direct a church choir, and play in dinner theaters and piano bars. New York–based pianist David Hahn says he makes over $51,000 annually by taking all kinds of gigs. Hahn plays at three church services a week for $100 each. This brings in $15,600 a year. He earns $31,200 from his teaching studio—he has twelve students who pay $50 a lesson every week. Hahn earns $3,000 a year playing background music at a department store once a month for $250. Additionally, he earns $1,200 a year playing two band gigs every month for $50 a gig. Hahn finds work by searching musical job boards on the Internet. He says that if musicians cannot find gigs in their hometowns, they should move to places like New York or Chicago, where they can find more work.

Working Conditions

One thing many professional musicians love about their job is that they do not have to set the alarm for work every morning. Most music gigs take place at night, or at least in late afternoon. The downside is that working in clubs and bars means playing until midnight or 1:00 a.m. (or even 4:00 a.m. in New Orleans, Las Vegas, or New York City). Then, equipment must be loaded for the drive home. As a result, some musicians go to bed when the sun is coming up and sleep past noon. Many gigs also occur on weekends. This can be especially stressful for musicians with families that keep more normal hours. Additionally, many bars are dirty, loud, smoky, and filled with people who have had too much to drink.

Earnings

The Bureau of Labor Statistics (BLS) states that musicians and singers earned an average wage of $24.20 an hour in 2015. The BLS notes that many who work in the field find only part-time or intermittent work. Those who work as orchestra musicians can earn from $30,000 to $125,000 a year, depending on where they live. These salaries reflect a full season of work—about forty weeks a year.

What Is the Future Outlook for Musicians?

The BLS says employment of musicians is expected to grow by only around 3 percent by 2024. That is slower than the 7 percent average growth for all occupations. The slow growth can be attributed to several factors. With the exploding popularity of electronic dance music, musicians find themselves competing with button-pushing disc jockeys for gigs. Moreover, people do not go out as much as they did in the past. Musicians are competing with the Internet, social media, digital downloads, and video streaming. On a brighter note, the demand for studio musicians who can record music for commercials, promotional websites, television shows, video games, and movies is expected to grow slightly faster than 3 percent in the coming decade.

Find Out More

Americana Music Association
PO Box 628
Franklin, TN 37065
website: http://americanamusic.org

This organization is dedicated to American roots music. It publishes newsletters, conducts market research, and disseminates information about important events in the Americana community that is of interest to musicians and students.

Careers in Music
PO Box 45362
Las Vegas, NV 89116
website: www.careersinmusic.com

This website features articles with career advice, listings of music schools, industry contacts, and numerous occupations that might be pursued by a professional musician.

MajoringInMusic.com
Box 2277
Boulder, CO 80306
website: www.majoringinmusic.com

This website provides information about music schools, summer music programs, scholarships, and other information a student needs to make smart decisions about majoring in music and establishing a sustainable career.

National Endowment for the Arts (NEA)
400 Seventh St. SW
Washington, DC 20506
website: www.arts.gov

The NEA is a federal agency that funds, promotes, and strengthens the creative arts. The organization supports performing ensembles, early music programs, music festivals, and youth orchestras.

Event Planner

What Does an Event Planner Do?

> **At a Glance**
> **Event Planner**
>
> **Minimum Educational Requirements**
> Bachelor's degree in hospitality management
>
> **Personal Qualities**
> Highly organized, good communicator, able to multitask
>
> **Certification and Licensing**
> A Certified Meeting Professional credential from the Convention Industry Council is voluntary but will help career advancement.
>
> **Working Conditions**
> Indoors in offices, hotels, restaurants, and convention centers; local and national travel is also sometimes required to visit venues.
>
> **Salary Range**
> Median pay of $46,840 in 2015
>
> **Number of Jobs**
> About 100,000 in 2015
>
> **Future Job Outlook**
> Projected growth of 10 percent by 2024 for meeting, convention, and event planners

Every day across the country, countless meetings, conventions, business and educational conferences, and other large-scale events take place. Most of these occasions are organized and supervised by event planners who manage every detail. Event planners work with clients to determine the time, place, theme, audience size, and cost of an event. They search for meeting sites such as convention centers and hotels and determine the quality of nearby lodging and services. Planners consider logistics like how easy it is to get to and from an event and what attractions are nearby that might interest visitors.

Planners contract with vendors who provide flowers, food, decorations, audiovisual equipment, and other necessities. They hire entertainers, bands, speakers, and interpreters and coordinate activities such as guest registration. Event planners work with caterers, wait staff, bartenders, and others to ensure that food is prepared and served smoothly and efficiently. When the event is over, planners pay vendors, coordinate cleanup, and meet with clients to obtain feedback. "You are putting on the event for other peoples' benefit, delight and objectives, you are there to do a job and not to enjoy yourself!" says Becki Cross, who has been planning events since 2004. As Cross wrote on the Event Manager website in 2015, "You are there to silently and efficiently work behind the scenes so that the event happens as if by magic."

Some event planners are specialists. Association planners are those who arrange annual industry conferences and trade shows for professional organizations such as the American Society of Civil Engineers or the Institute of Food Technologists. Marketing is part of the job; association planners try to find the most desirable locations and make the events as exciting as possible to attract the largest number of people.

Convention service managers work for hotels, convention centers, and other meeting facilities. These managers work with professional associations, government groups, and businesses that require event facilities. Convention service managers work with other event planners to determine budgets, food choices, and other options. Corporate planners work for a single company. They coordinate the event and meeting needs within a corporation and schedule online conferences and other events. Nonprofit event planners work with charities and advocacy organizations. They specialize in banquets, food drives, and charity events held to raise money for various causes.

Wedding planners are the most well-known event planners. These specialists work with a bride, groom, and relatives to plan wedding themes, food, music, flowers, and countless other details. However, wedding planners also handle other events, such as reunions, anniversaries, religious celebrations, galas, ceremonies, and social events.

Most people do not realize the size of the meetings and events industry. The industry generates $485 billion in the United States every year and employs over 1.7 million people. It has a bigger economic impact than that of the auto manufacturing and airline industries. The reason the industry is so large is due to an old-fashioned concept; face-to-face contacts remain important in business, even in today's fast-paced world of texting and videoconferencing. As event planners understand, business events are not parties. "[People] attending meetings and events are not there to enjoy the complementary shrimp and score a goodie-filled bling bag," event planner Victoria Pynchon told *Forbes* magazine in 2011. "Networking at events lays the groundwork for serious business deals, some of which are actually signed and sealed right there in the exhibit hall."

How Do You Become an Event Planner?

Education

In the past many event planners did not have special training. However, the nature of the work has become more complex in recent years, and employers now prefer candidates who have a bachelor's degree in hospitality management. Course work for this degree focuses on a wide range of subjects, including hotel management, meeting and event management, marketing, public relations, food production, cost control and analysis, and business communications. Event planner applicants who do not hold a bachelor's degree are expected to have at least one to two years' experience working in the field.

Certification and Licensing

Event planners who obtain certification will have an easier time finding a job and a better chance to advance in the industry. Certification is voluntary and is available in several specialized fields. A Certified Meeting Professional (CMP) credential from the Convention Industry Council (CIC) is available to convention, meeting, and exhibition planners. The CIC also offers the CMP-HC certification for event planners in the health care industry. Both CIC certification programs require applicants to prove that they have had three years of experience and have recently worked in the industry. They must also pass a written exam that covers various facets of event planning.

The Society of Government Meeting Professionals certifies those who work with local, state, or federal government agencies. The Certified Government Meeting Professional (CGMP) certification requires applicants to take a three-day course and pass an exam that covers government travel regulations, purchasing policies, and other relevant issues. Those who wish to obtain a CGMP certification must be members of the Society of Government Meeting Professionals for six months and work as an event planner for at least one year.

Wedding planners have several options for certification offered by the American Association of Certified Wedding Planners, the Association of Certified Professional Wedding Consultants, and others.

Volunteer Work and Internships

Many prospective event planners gain vital experience by offering their time and services for free. Local charities are always looking for volunteers to help plan fund-raisers, charity runs, and other events. Students can volunteer to plan school fund-raisers and banquets for sports teams. Those interested in this career can also seek advice from professional planners to ask them about their business, education, and experience. "Let the event planner know you are interested in joining the field and you may be surprised at how helpful they will be," event planner Holly Jacoby wrote on EventPlanning.com in 2012. "Ask for their business card so you can reach out to them later and see if they are looking for an intern."

Skills and Personality

Most successful event planners are perfectionists. They often deal with powerful clients—and even celebrities—who expect every aspect of an event to be excellent. Event planners must also be skilled multitaskers. At any given moment during an event, they are talking to clients, guests, and vendors, all with their own sets of problems and requests. On the career planning website the Muse, Elizabeth Conway, who plans events for a venture capital firm, offers advice to prospective event planners. "Don't get into this field unless you're the person that organizes every happy hour, plans every trip with friends, color coordinates your closet, and gets pleasure out of making a to-do list," she says. "It's not all about picking out tablecloths and flowers; it's a lot of data and detail, too."

Good communication skills are required for this job. Event planners often find themselves giving orders to many people at once, in person, on the phone, and via text and e-mail. It takes a high degree of organization to react calmly under pressure and make good decisions when surrounded by people who are stressed out. Event planners also work long hours, as event planner Alison Kasko explained on the QC Event School website in 2016. "You'll usually be the first to arrive at a venue, and the last to leave," she says. "That means you could be crawling into bed late into the night or waking up during the early hours of the morning. But this flexibility is also what makes becoming an event planner so exciting; you essentially run your own show."

Victoria Pynchon said that event planners must be ready for anything, especially when working to coordinate a large event that has many moving pieces. "I don't know one successful meeting planner or any other professional, who hasn't found herself in a do-or-die, make-it-work situation," she said. "At one point or another, the attendees get there, the caterer has an emergency, or the venue floods and you just have to set your expectations free and think on your feet."

On the Job

Employers

In 2015 there were about one hundred thousand jobs for meeting, convention, and event planners. Most event planners work for private companies in the business sector. About 20 percent work for professional, civic, or religious organizations. About 15 percent plan events for the lodging and food service industry. Around 10 percent of event planners are self-employed.

Working Conditions

While event planners usually use their office as a base of operations, they are often on the move. Travel is sometimes required to plan events that take place in distant cities and even exotic locations. If a planner is working on a large event like a job fair, national convention, film screening, or annual conference, they will travel to the client's location. Planning an event entails visiting attendees and vendors and inspecting convention centers, restaurants, and other venues. To Jennifer Carver, who has planned events for nine years for the University of Southern California, all this adds up to an exciting job. "I wanted a career that was fast-paced where I would be doing something different each day and not stuck behind a desk 40 hours a week," as she said on the Muse website in 2016. "Event planning allows you to work on such a wide variety of projects and no two are exactly the same. Even if you're planning an annual event, it's always a challenge to continue to improve it and make it better than it was the year before."

Earnings

According to the Bureau of Labor Statistics (BLS), event planners who worked full time earned a median wage of $46,840 in 2015. The lowest-paid 10 percent earned less than $25,680, and the highest-paid 10 percent earned more than $82,050.

Opportunities for Advancement

Event planners might start out as an administrative assistant who plans events in addition to other duties or as a caterer or manager of a hotel or restaurant. They can start out as a conference coordinator and move up to higher-paying positions like meeting manager or executive director of event planning. Some event planners become self-employed consultants or start their own companies.

What Is the Future Outlook for Event Planners?

According to the BLS, the number of people working as event planners is expected to grow by 10 percent through 2024. The most populous states—California, New York, Texas, and Florida—have the greatest number of event planners.

In the coming years industry growth will be driven by globalization, as companies open offices in different countries. Event planners will likely find work scheduling corporate events that allow regionally, nationally, or internationally assigned employees to meet face-to-face.

Find Out More

Association of Certified Professional Wedding Consultants (ACPWC)
122 Destry Ct.
San Jose, CA 95136
website: www.acpwc.org

The ACPWC is dedicated to professionalizing the wedding planner industry. The organization offers training and certification for wedding consultants, event planners, facility coordinators, and students. The site provides networking, referrals, and support to members.

Convention Industry Council (CIC)
700 N. Fairfax St., Suite 510
Alexandria, VA 22314
website: www.conventionindustry.org

The CIC is the leading organization for the meetings, conventions, and exhibition industry. Its website provides access to the CMP industry certification program. The CMP Career Center features sample interview questions, job descriptions, job listings, and information about hiring.

Professional Convention Management Association (PCMA)
35 E. Wacker Dr., Suite 500
Chicago, IL 60601
website: www.pcma.org

The PCMA specializes in education, networking, and community engagement organization for planners of meetings, conventions, and business events. The organization sponsors an education foundation that funds grants, scholarships, and research programs. The site also features job listings.

Society of Government Meeting Professionals (SGMP)
3337 Duke St.
Alexandria, VA 22314
website: www.sgmp.org

The SGMP website caters to government meeting professionals who work with various agencies to provide cost-effective, high-quality government meetings. The organization offers numerous training programs, webinars, and educational resources.

Talent Scout

What Does a Talent Scout Do?

> **At a Glance**
> ### Talent Scout
> **Minimum Educational Requirements**
> Bachelor's degree in music, film, communications, business, or marketing
>
> **Personal Qualities**
> Passionate about music, film, or modeling; ability to spot talent; strong negotiating skills; hardworking; loyal; determined
>
> **Certification and Licensing**
> States such as California and Florida require special talent agency licenses for anyone who procures employment for artists.
>
> **Working Conditions**
> Hectic schedules, including nights and weekends attending plays, openings, concerts, and other entertainment events
>
> **Salary Range**
> Median pay of $54,000 in 2015
>
> **Number of Jobs**
> About 13,230 in 2015
>
> **Future Job Outlook**
> Projected growth of nearly 5 percent by 2024

Every day, thousands of people pursue their dream of becoming famous. They take lessons in acting, dancing, and singing and go to auditions known as "cattle calls," which often attract dozens of hopefuls. But some well-known actors and entertainers did not follow the standard Hollywood formula to riches and fame. They were discovered by talent scouts who picked them out of a crowd.

For example, a modeling scout spotted future actor Channing Tatum as he walked down a Miami street. Tatum was handed the equivalent of a winning lottery ticket. The talent scout got Tatum work as a model in print ads for the Gap. Tatum went on to appear in TV commercials, music videos, and eventually blockbuster films like *Magic Mike XXL* and *The Hateful Eight*. Similarly, singer Toni Braxton was discovered by a record scout one day as she sang to herself while filling her car up with gas.

Actress Charlize Theron was also discovered by a Hollywood talent scout named John Crosby, who heard her loudly arguing with a bank teller who refused to cash her check. Crosby was struck by Theron's manner and appearance, and he got her a role in a horror movie.

Talent scouts seek out exceptional people at theaters, comedy clubs, music clubs, fashion shows, and other entertainment venues. They search through videos on YouTube and other social media platforms looking for people who have unique abilities. Many talent scouts are former performers or musicians who have connections and experience in the entertainment industry. Scouts negotiate contracts for their clients, ensure that clients get paid for their work, and deduct a percentage of the pay as a commission.

Successful talent scouts have personal relationships with TV and film talent agents. Agents represent the business interests of their clients; their job involves getting clients work and managing their careers. Every day, talent agents receive dozens of unsolicited submissions from those hoping to break into the business. Actors mail out letters, résumés, and publicity photos called head shots. Most end up in the trash. A good scout can bypass this process and help an actor, writer, musician, or composer get an interview with an agent. Scouts also convince agents to attend a play, view a screening, or otherwise go to an event to showcase their clients' work. "Approaching agents and managers can be daunting—we're the middle-man," said talent scout Ryan J-W Smith of his profession on the Talent Scout website in 2016. "[We] help you understand exactly how the market works in your city and how best to fine-tune your online presence to make powerful agents and managers not just sit up and take notice, but fight each other to sign you."

Scouts who specialize in music are known as artists and repertoire representatives, or A&R reps. A&R reps work in the A&R division of a record label or music publishing company. Reps seek out undiscovered recording artists and songwriters and work with them to develop their talents. Traditionally, reps acted as a link between artists and their record label. The rep convinced a record label to sign a contract with the client, found a record producer, and helped promote and market the client.

However, the role of the A&R rep has changed since the early twenty-first century. Musicians can now record their work on their own using a smartphone, laptop, or desktop computer and promote it via social media. In addition, there are not as many major record companies as there used to be. However, A&R reps are still out scouting for new talent. Andrew Corria is an A&R rep at Aftermath Entertainment. In a 2016 interview on the Careers in Music website, Corria said his job involves "finding artists and new talent, overseeing the current musical project, [finding] anything that would be a good fit for a song on [the project] . . . recruiting musical talent—whether it's producers, artists or musicians." Corria discovered several of his most popular acts on the music-sharing site SoundCloud. He also checks out music blogs and song posts on social networking sites.

Model scouts are specialists who focus on the fashion industry. It is their job to discover and recruit aspiring models. They work to connect their clients with modeling agencies, advertising agencies, production companies, and photographers. Scouts schedule meetings between models and clients, coordinate the details of a project (such as location and wardrobe), and ensure the model is prepared on the day of the shoot.

How Do You Become a Talent Scout?

Education

There are no educational requirements to be a talent scout, but the field is highly competitive. Entertainment companies prefer applicants who have bachelor's degrees in music, film, communications, marketing, or business. Some colleges offer specific music business or film business courses. These programs can help prospective scouts get the foundation and skills they need, along with a foot in the door at a production company or record label after they graduate.

Many talent scouts began their careers in the fields they now scout. Music talent scouts gain experience working as musicians, club disc jockeys, or music bookers. Some find employment at a record company. Many model scouts originally worked as models or model agents. Prospective acting scouts might have first acted in community theater or worked at a studio. While not everyone has the necessary skills or talents to work as actors, models, or musicians, this is a great way to learn the business from the inside.

Certification and Licensing

Over the years talent scouts have been known to engage in a variety of scams. Some charge unsuspecting clients up-front fees before they do any work, or they charge large sums to provide acting classes and arrange for head shots. Some scammers even recruit innocent would-be actors for pornographic films. Because of the trade's notoriously dishonest element, California, Florida, Texas, and other states require anyone who procures work for artists to be licensed. License requirements vary from state to state. In California prospective talent agents must supply the labor bureau with sample contracts, character references, and various legal documentation. License requirements have not stopped all the scammers. But a client can have more trust in a scout who holds an official state talent agent license.

Volunteer Work and Internships

Experience is the best teacher, and prospective talent scouts should be willing to work for free to gain knowledge in the field. Scouts often begin their careers volunteering in the local film, theater, music, or modeling scene. Volunteers get hands-on experience helping local talent with bookings, promotions, tours, and other projects. This allows them to network with actors, models, musicians, writers, composers, producers, directors, and others who can help them make industry connections.

Film studios offer internships in various positions involving marketing, publicity, and business. Production interns help those who are producing movies. People who land these internships are well positioned to move on to work as casting assistants and casting directors. These jobs provide invaluable experience for a prospective acting scout. Another path for acting scouts is to volunteer for a position at a local community theater. This provides experience working with producers, directors, and actors and helps build a network of business contacts.

Skills and Personality

The most important skill for any scout is to have the ability to see potential in an undiscovered artist; to recognize and cultivate talent and know whether an artist is marketable. Scouts have an in-depth understanding of what works and what does not, as well as what type of talent will make an impact on consumers and broader culture. These skills are honed by having an obsessive interest in the entertainment industry. Typical A&R reps closely follow music and the music business; they search out new sounds, read trade journals, check out videos on the Internet, and regularly go to clubs and bars to scout new talent. An acting scout will take the same approach to the TV and movie business; watching and analyzing dozens of new productions, reading about the industry, attending plays and openings, and meeting actors at auditions and other entertainment venues.

Talent scouts must also have strong business and sales skills. They need to approach artists, sell them on their abilities as a scout, and negotiate the best business deals for their clients. As Andrew Corria puts it, "You're there to get what you need from them and they're there to get what they need from you."

It is also necessary to have good communication skills and a thick skin. Scouts act as intermediaries between impulsive artists and jaded producers, bored engineers, and cynical project managers. They sometimes work around the clock to smooth out messy relationships and go the extra mile to expedite a deal.

On the Job

Employers

A talent scout might be self-employed or work for a record label, publishing company, or film, TV, or commercial production studio. Some scouts are employed by talent agencies. Reputable talent agencies have good industry connections and are licensed by state governments.

Working Conditions

Working conditions depend on a scout's chosen field, but the job rarely involves nine-to-five office work. Those who work in TV or film get paid to attend plays, film openings, and other industry gatherings. They sit through casting meetings and auditions, visit studios and soundstages, and spend hours sending e-mails and texts and participating in conference calls.

In the music business, nothing much happens before late afternoon. As a result, many A&R reps work the "night shift." They get up late, take afternoon meetings, and visit clubs, recording studios, and other musician haunts at night. Schedules can be hectic. A rep might deal with office paperwork during the day and attend a jam session until the wee hours of the night. This is not a job for someone who likes to be in bed by 11:00 p.m. and sleep nine hours every night.

Earnings

Talent scouts usually receive 10 percent of their client's earnings. The average annual wage for a talent scout in 2015 was $54,000. However, wages often depend on the scout's experience and commitment to the job. Someone just starting out might earn as little as $10,000 a year, while those who have discovered major talents can bring in as much as $150,000 annually.

Opportunities for Advancement

Talent scouts often begin their careers working menial jobs at talent agencies, record companies, and film studios. They fetch coffee, sort mail, and file papers. With hard work and perseverance, they can advance to positions such as assistant and eventually agent. This can provide a background for the scout to become self-employed. A freelance scout might start small, booking talent for local commercials or music clubs, and then move on to work with major studios. As talent scouts discover a larger number of rising stars, their portfolio of clients grows along with their connections in the industry. If a scout develops a good enough reputation, he or she might be recruited to work for a big Hollywood studio like Warner Bros. or Twentieth Century Fox.

What Is the Future Outlook for Talent Scouts?

The Bureau of Labor Statistics (BLS) does not have a specific category for talent scouts. But according to the BLS, employment opportunities for agents and business managers of artists and performers are expected to grow by almost 5 percent by 2024.

New opportunities for scouts are expected to come from nontraditional sources. Online companies like Amazon, Netflix, and Hulu are producing a growing number of original programs. These companies are working with talent scouts to bring fresh faces and unique talents to their producers.

Find Out More

Association of Talent Agents (ATA)
9255 Sunset Blvd., Suite 930
Los Angeles, CA 90069
website: www.agentassociation.com

The ATA has been the official trade association for talent agents since 1937. Prospective talent agents will find useful information on the association website, such as laws relating to talent agencies, as well as links to entertainment guilds, unions, and organizations such as the Motion Picture Association of America.

Fox Internship Program
website: https://foxcareers.com

21st Century Fox offers internships to students at its numerous entertainment companies, including Twentieth Century Fox Film, Twentieth Century Fox Television, Fox Networks Group, and Fox Entertainment Group. Prospective talent scouts can gain practical experience carrying out daily tasks and participating in development workshops.

Los Angeles Film School

6363 Sunset Blvd.
Hollywood, CA 90028
website: www.lafil.edu

The Los Angeles Film School offers associate's and bachelor's degrees in majors relating to the entertainment industry. Students wishing to pursue a career as a talent scout can learn about the inner workings of the film industry.

Warner Bros. Careers: Internships

website: www.warnerbroscareers.com

Summer internships at Warner Bros. are for students currently enrolled in an accredited undergraduate or graduate program. A prospective talent scout can learn many different aspects of the business, including marketing, social media, publicity, creative development, finance, digital media, and media research.

Disc Jockey

What Does a Disc Jockey Do?

The business magazine *Forbes* calls disc jockey (DJ) superstars Calvin Harris, Tiësto, and Skrillex the "Electronic Cash Kings." Between the three of them, these electronic dance music (EDM) DJs generated over $121 million in 2016. There are plenty of other DJs also earning tens of millions of dollars a year. However, like any branch of the entertainment business, for every cash king or queen, there are thousands who struggle to break into the business. The DJ one sees spinning tunes at a wedding or event probably has dreams of becoming the next Diplo. It is not hard to see why; writing and mixing songs and performing them in front of thousands of adoring fans might be one of the best jobs in the entertainment business.

> ### At a Glance
> ### Disc Jockey
>
> **Minimum Educational Requirements**
> None
>
> **Personal Qualities**
> Musical talent, obsessive interest in music, technical ability, communication and marketing skills
>
> **Certification and Licensing**
> None required
>
> **Working Conditions**
> Indoors in bars, clubs, banquet halls, and concert venues
>
> **Salary Range**
> Median pay of $26,930 in 2015, but some superstars earn millions
>
> **Number of Jobs**
> About 53,000 in 2015
>
> **Future Job Outlook**
> Projected growth of 3 percent by 2025

Whether they are playing tracks at a local club or for EDM music lovers at the Ultra Music Festival, DJs select songs, manipulate the tunes with various electronic tools, and mix them into unique sounds that feature propulsive dance beats. Some write and sing their own songs and record them on computers

A disc jockey spins tunes at a club. DJs select, mix, and write songs; during performances, they use synthesizers, guitars, drums, sequencers, and other tools of their trade.

using synthesizers, guitars, drums, and other instruments. DJs also use digital music sequencers that can produce unusual noises and re-create the sounds of pianos, horns, drums, and other instruments. Sequencers allow DJs to record, edit, and manipulate the pitch and scale of notes using filters and effects. A sequencer can sample, or take a portion of a previously recorded song, and reuse it as a melody in a different song. Some DJs add visual spectacle to their performances by dressing in imaginative costumes and masks, using laser lights, and enhancing their act with other eye candy.

DJs work in a variety of venues, and these often determine their style and brand of music. Those who work at nightclubs or bars play specific styles meant to cater to the tastes of the audience. Some clubs feature individual EDM genres like dubstep, house, or garage. The job of a club DJ is to keep people dancing without interruption. This means blending together long songs and ramping the energy up and down to keep listeners interested. The work is attractive to many because club DJs can earn good money, attract intense fans, and gain a great deal of notoriety. As author Hillegonda C. Rietveld wrote in her 2013 book *DJ Culture in the Mix*, the DJ is a "party leader, sonic entertainer, auditory artist, music programmer, record mixer, beat-matcher, cultural masher, music producer, creative music archivist, record collector . . . witch-doctor, [and] shaman."

A different type of sonic entertainer, called a mobile DJ, works weddings, family reunions, and other celebrations. Mobile DJs play requests—and sometimes entire playlists—for people at parties. They act as master of ceremonies, speaking into a microphone to work the crowd. A mobile DJ might introduce the bride and groom, shout out to other guests, and encourage people to get up and dance. In 2011 wedding DJ Michael M. Hughes described his job on the Digital DJ Tips website: "[I play] for crowds of fifty to three-hundred, aged 3 to 103, from every social strata, with musical preferences ranging from The Hokey Pokey to Eric Clapton to Skrillex . . . all of them itching to burn off their roast beef and mashed potatoes dancing nonstop until the event manager tells you to pull the plug."

Radio DJs are in an entirely different category of DJ. They play songs on the air, announce the weather and news, and play commercials. DJs are supervised by music directors who pick the songs that are played on the radio. This makes a radio DJ's job very structured, as New Jersey DJ Laurie Cataldo explained in 2012 on the radio station website 94.3 The Point: "I talk after the first song. I play 2 songs, talk again, then play another song. Then commercials, ending with the weather. After weather is a song, then I talk, play 2 songs, talk, play 2 songs, talk, play one song . . . then more commercials."

How Do You Become a Disc Jockey?

Education

Before he was famous, Swedish DJ Aviici spent up to ten hours a day in his bedroom with CD turntables and effects boxes, recording songs on his laptop. After winning a DJ competition on BBC Radio in the United Kingdom, Aviici was approached by a manager who wanted to make him a superstar. There was just one problem. The eighteen-year-old Aviici was a bedroom DJ; he had no idea what it was that club

DJs did in the sound booth. Aviici's manager hired two professional DJs who spent eighteen months teaching him how to spin tunes and work the crowd.

Aviici was lucky; budding DJs are not usually backed by enthusiastic managers. Most DJs who want to make the leap from the bedroom to the club have to learn the tricks of the trade on their own or take classes. Schools such as Dubspot and Scratch DJ Academy, both located in New York City, have good reputations and have achieved wide acclaim in the entertainment industry. Some schools offer an associate of science in music production program, which teaches students basics like music theory, composition, audio engineering, audio software training, record mastering, and digital music production. Students get hands-on experience mixing music on laptops using software like Logic Pro and Ableton Live. On his personal website, a blogger and DJ known as Turningthetable describes the benefits of taking digital music courses: "DJ schools often have big name DJs guest teach during lectures, feature state-of-the-art equipment in their classrooms and host technology-driven courses to help ensure you're a certified DJ once everything is completed."

DJs who hope to turn their love of music into a career should also learn about communications, business, and finance as it pertains to the music industry. Building a DJ business involves a major investment. A basic sound package with computers, software, microphones, sequencers, speakers, effects boxes, amplifiers, and other necessary equipment can cost $10,000. To be successful, DJs also need to be entrepreneurs. They have to find gigs, promote their services in ads on social media, and keep track of contracts and invoices, as well as taking care of other bookkeeping tasks.

DJ schools can cost anywhere from $1,000 to $5,000, and there is no guarantee that the courses will lead to gigs. That is why most DJs are self-taught. They network with other amateurs to learn and watch how-to videos on the web. But as any professional musician will agree, experience is the greatest teacher. "If you want to be taken seriously as a DJ, you need to play *live*, for *real living, breathing humans*," says Michael M. Hughes. "And the best schooling you can get is not found on YouTube, or expensive online mixing courses, or in getting a bunch of Likes on your Facebook page. It's playing for crowds."

Certification and Licensing

DJ schools offer certificates to students who successfully complete their courses. Images of these certificates can be posted on a DJ's website to inspire confidence in prospective customers. But as Turningthetable explains, "a school-issued DJ certificate is not necessary for any professional (or amateur, for that matter) gigs. Unlike degrees from universities and colleges, a DJ certificate is not a true measure of how capable a [person] is in his or her respective medium."

Volunteer Work and Internships

DJs who are just starting their careers often take any gigs they can get. They play for free at parties and events to gain experience and fans. Playing different types of gigs can also help a DJ decide what sort of career to pursue. Some prefer to do weddings, as they are a good source of regular income. Others might want to work their way up through the nightclubs with the goal of rising to the top of their profession. Whatever the gig, playing a lot of them is the best way to network, learn about the industry, and gain experience twiddling the knobs. On his personal website PassionateDJ.com, club DJ David Michael explains that he gained experience by offering his music for free. "My approach was to go to a struggling night club and offer to promote my own event series," he says. "I ran a monthly Thursday night for about a year. It wasn't a raging success. But, it got me used to club DJing, hooking up to a real PA, and small-scale promotion."

Skills and Personality

Most DJs start out as obsessive music fans. They study musical genres, listen to other DJs on music-sharing sites like SoundCloud, watch DJ videos, and go to clubs and concerts to see live performances. Successful mobile DJs have a solid understanding of what musical styles and songs people want to hear at weddings, including genres like Motown, 1980s and 1990s rock, disco, new wave, and pop ballads. Hughes offers these words: "Successful DJs share the same qualities as all successful entertainers—polished interpersonal skills, proven technical ability, effective marketing—but uniquely and most importantly, he or she possesses an instinctive understanding of how to work a crowd and how to play precisely the right song at precisely the right time."

On the Job

Employers

Most DJs are self-employed self-promoters. They record demonstration records, or demos, to get gigs from bar owners, concert promoters, and wedding planners. DJs with a measure of success often work with agents and managers who book gigs, handle negotiations, and deal with contracts and promotion.

Working Conditions

DJs work at bars, clubs, concert halls, banquet halls, private parties, and even on cruise ships. DJs get to listen to music all the time and get paid to play for adoring fans. But being a DJ is not all about glamour, and there are negative aspects to the job. Any professional DJ will admit that a nightclub is not the healthiest environment. People drink, smoke, and can become loud and aggressive. Party promoters and bar owners do not always honor their commitments, and sometimes DJs do not get the money they were promised. Excessive travel can also be difficult. "I would cram in as many cities as I could," British DJ Annie Mac told the online magazine *Thump* in a 2013 interview. "They were tough tours. You would be lucky to break even, but they were such an adventure. . . . It was always unpredictable and despite jet-lag, delirium and sometimes chronic loneliness, always interesting."

Earnings

The average annual salary for a DJ in 2015 was $26,930, according to the career website Sokanu. The average pay for a radio DJs was slightly more—$35,080 in 2015. A wedding DJ can earn a much better wage. While beginners start out earning around $200 to $300 for a four-hour wedding, experienced professionals who work full time can earn $1,000 to $2,500 per gig.

Opportunities for Advancement

Some club DJs generate enough interest that they can move up to the role of performer or guest DJ. These DJs build a reputation for themselves and attract fans who come specifically to see them perform. DJs who develop a large enough following can play in bigger clubs for better pay. Some top clubs pay tens of thousands of dollars a night to book their star record spinners.

What Is the Future Outlook for DJs?

The Bureau of Labor Statistics (BLS) does not have a category for DJs, but the career website Sokanu estimates the field will grow by about 3 percent overall by 2025. However, those who work as EDM DJs may find more opportunities; according to *Forbes*, the EDM industry generated $6.9 billion in 2015—50 percent more than in 2013. This is good news for EDM DJs, since the number of establishments featuring this style of music continues to grow.

Find Out More

American Disc Jockey Association (ADJA)
20118 N. Sixty-Seventh Ave., Suite 300-605
Glendale, AZ 85308
website: www.adja.org

The ADJA sponsors special events like Mobile Beat Las Vegas and provides useful information for DJs and prospective DJs, such as job listings and educational seminars.

Dubspot
138 Fifth Ave.
New York, NY 10011
website: www.dubspot.com

The website for the New York City–based school offers online courses in DJ equipment and software, job opportunities, and a chance for students to earn a producer certificate.

EDM Jobs

540 Howard St.
San Francisco, CA 94105
website: www.edmjobs.com

This website contains hundreds of job listings in the electronic music industry for DJs, writers, managers, marketers, and more.

Los Angeles Recording School

6363 Sunset Blvd.
Hollywood, CA 90028
website: http://learn.lafilm.edu/music-production

The Los Angeles Recording School offers an eighteen-month associate of science in music production program that focuses on the latest digital music production technology. Courses include music theory, composition, mixing, and mastering.

SoundCloud

website: https://soundcloud.com

Superstar DJs such as Aviici and Skrillex began their careers posting music on SoundCloud and continue to do so even today. The site enables users to upload, record, promote, and share their original music and is a musical storehouse for over 40 million users. Prospective DJs can listen to every genre and style and find inspiration in the work of others.

Makeup Artist

What Does a Makeup Artist Do?

At a Glance
Makeup Artist

Minimum Educational Requirements
None, but cosmetology school will open doors to better opportunities

Personal Qualities
A passion for hair and makeup, good business and communications skills, hard worker, self-promoter

Certification and Licensing
Many states require makeup artists to acquire a license.

Working Conditions
Indoors on film and television sets, backstage at theaters, in trailers when working on movie locations

Salary Range
Median pay of $53,230 in 2015

Number of Jobs
About 3,060 in 2015

Future Job Outlook
Projected growth of 10 percent by 2024 for all makeup artists, hair stylists, and cosmetologists

Nearly every person who appears on TV or in a movie—whether a news anchor or a superstar celebrity—is wearing stage makeup and other cosmetics. These beauty products were applied by a makeup artist moments before the scene was shot. Makeup artists specialize in enhancing actors' beauty to make them appear flawless on screen. They use cosmetics and skilled application techniques to bring out a client's best features. Makeup artists highlight certain areas of the face, cover imperfections, and help improve the look of an actor's complexion.

Some makeup artists work with a special effect called prosthetics, which includes fake blood and silicone rubber body parts. These professionals are known as special effects makeup artists. They use their skills to make actors look like monsters, angels, zombies, aliens, and other fantasy creatures. Special effects makeup artists also make actors look as if they were shot, cut, bruised, bloodied, and injured in numerous other horrible ways.

Whatever their specialty, the job of the makeup artist is to make characters look as realistic as possible. As Hollywood producer Phil Breman explained on the financial website the Balance in 2016: "As an audience member, assuming all other elements are met (acting, writing, directing), it becomes that much easier for you to become invested in the characters on the screen when the make up is done well. It is a true artistry."

Expert makeup artists are also important to actors who need to have their appearance altered or enhanced; having good makeup makes it easier for an actor to commit to the role. Actor Ralph Fiennes spent nearly three hours in a makeup chair every day so a makeup artist could transform him into Lord Voldemort for the *Harry Potter* movies. Fiennes told MTV it helped him get into character. "A certain look that you have helps you locate who you're being," he said.

A makeup artist prepares a client for her on-screen appearance. Whether the goal is to help an actor look his or her best or to create convincing fantasy creatures, makeup artists must be familiar with all sorts of cosmetics and how best to apply them.

"You look at yourself in the mirror, you see this face, and you say, 'I know who I am.'"

Makeup artists work with lipstick, lip liner, mascara, eye shadow, eyeliner, artificial eyelashes, foundation, hair spray, concealer, bronzer, hydrating creams, skin pore lotions, and powder. Their tools include brushes for applying makeup, eyebrow pencils, and applicators for blemishes.

Special effects makeup artists work with liquid latex, a skin-colored liquid. It can be applied in layers and built up to form skin-like textures that resemble scars, wounds, and physical deformities. Liquid latex is also poured into molds made from modeling clay. This is used to make facial prosthetics, which can make an actor appear very old or monstrous. A special glue called spirit gum is used to stick prosthetics to an actor's body. Special effects makeup artist Peter Zunitch explained the various questions he needs to consider when doing makeup. As he told *Videomaker* magazine in October 2014: "Will the makeup be seen close up or from far away? Will the talent be required to 'act' through the makeup and to what extent? What will the lighting and costuming look like? Will the genre be silly or serious? If the appliance is required over many days can you recreate it with speed and accuracy?"

When working on film and TV sets, makeup artists usually work as part of a team. The team consists of a chief makeup artist, or makeup designer, who oversees the entire makeup department. Chief makeup artists design looks for each character, assign tasks to individual makeup artists, and supervise all work.

The makeup supervisor hires and manages the hair and makeup teams on a production. He or she orders supplies, manages budgets, and ensures production schedules are followed. Supervisors also oversee screen tests to see how makeup, special effects, and hair fittings will appear on the screen. Supervisors also ensure what is called continuity: the requirement that an actor's makeup look exactly the same from scene to scene.

Makeup assistants help makeup artists. Assistants apply makeup, do touch-ups, and help actors remove makeup. They get supplies, handle phone calls and texts, and do whatever else is necessary to make the artist's job easier.

How Do You Become a Makeup Artist?

Education

Makeup artists face the same challenge as many others hoping to break into the entertainment business; there is a lot of competition for a small number of jobs. Those who attend cosmetology school might have better odds landing one of those coveted positions. Sometimes referred to as "beauty" school, cosmetology school is where students learn the fundamental skills of hair and skin care and makeup application. They also learn how to run a business and how to market their services. Some schools offer special courses in film and television makeup and special effects makeup. They also offer opportunities for prospective makeup artists to network with industry insiders.

Most makeup artists will say that continuous self-education is important throughout their career. They familiarize themselves with a wide variety of products, keep up with changing trends and fashions, and watch a lot of movies to study the work of others in the field.

Certification and Licensing

Many states require makeup artists to obtain what is called an esthetician's license. (*Esthetician* is another word for beautician or skin care specialist.) However, laws vary from state to state. For example, Colorado requires makeup artists to be licensed estheticians. Connecticut law does not mention makeup artists specifically but requires cosmetologists who provide face and hair beauty treatments to be licensed. Even California—the center of the entertainment industry—is rather confusing when it comes to licensing requirements. If individuals provide makeup services at weddings, salons, or spas, they must have a state-certified esthetician license. This requires the holder to complete at least six hundred hours of course work and training from an accredited school in the state. However, those who work as freelance makeup artists do not need a California esthetician license. The laws are similar in New York, where numerous TV shows and films are produced. Freelance makeup artists who work in New York do not need a license. Those who work in salons, however, must obtain six hundred hours of course work and training to receive an esthetician license.

Volunteer Work and Internships

Many makeup artists begin their careers as interns who participate in the production of student or independent films or volunteer for community theater productions. This sort of work is a way to gain valuable experience, as makeup artist Karla Powell blogs on Tumblr: "I always tell other aspiring make-up artists to assist local makeup artists & get as much work experience as you can! You see the good, bad and everything that way then."

Skills and Personality

Because many makeup artists are freelancers, they must be self-motivated and good at self-promotion. Makeup artists need business skills to handle contracts, keep track of invoices, and negotiate with clients. They must also be hard workers. The job often entails working nights and weekends and might include twelve- or even eighteen-hour days on a film set.

Since most scenes in a film are shot out of sequence, makeup artists need to be perfectionists. They must be able to re-create a specific look so a character's appearance is exactly the same in every scene. This requires many hours of off-duty preparation; makeup artists must constantly practice to improve their artistry. They typically try out different looks on themselves and on their friends. "Practice is key," says cosmetology teacher Simone Ciafardini on the beauty tips website Makeup Tutorials. "Learning from professionals is important to becoming a truly great artist, but making practice part of your everyday routine is also critical."

Since television and movie production is a team effort, makeup artists must be good listeners who can clearly communicate with stylists, set designers, lighting technicians, producers, directors, and performers. The job also requires a high degree of commitment; makeup artists spend a considerable amount of time "off the clock" researching and developing makeup that will be required for an upcoming production. This includes studying elaborate makeup techniques that might be necessary for costume dramas, horror films, or science fiction movies.

On the Job

Employers

Makeup artists work with photographers and television, movie, and theatrical producers. Their clients include models, actors, musicians, and extras who play minor roles in many productions. Some makeup artists work weddings, making brides and their wedding parties look and feel beautiful on their special day. Some begin their careers working behind makeup counters at a local department store, where they can get experience working on people of all ages and skin types.

Working Conditions

Makeup artists who do weddings or work for personal clients often work weekends and night hours. Those who work in TV and movies often complain about the long hours. Film shoots might begin at the break of dawn and continue well past midnight. The work can carry on at a hectic pace or grind to a halt as new shots are set up. As makeup artist Malia Miglino writes in *Ms.* magazine: "There has never been one time when things went at a comfortable pace. Get used to being uncomfortable. . . . You usually have too many [actors] to do in an incredibly small amount of time OR you have one actor every 6 hours."

Makeup artists who work in the entertainment business often travel to film shoots in exotic or remote locations. They might be exposed to wind, dust, rain, snow, intense sun, and extreme temperatures when working on location. For example, the TV show *Fargo* was shot in Alberta, Canada, in the middle of winter. Chief makeup artist Gail Kennedy spent her workdays in a fur hat and kept her makeup bag under her heavy down coat to keep the lotions from freezing. "The makeup crew is careful not to apply anything that might freeze on the skin," she told *Variety* magazine in 2016. "We're fast with our [makeup] resets so the actors can finish their scenes and get into the warmth. Adhesives don't react the same way in dry cold, either. That was particularly challenging with all of the facial hairpieces."

Earnings

Compensation for makeup artists varies greatly, depending on the position. The Bureau of Labor Statistics (BLS) says that cosmetologists and makeup artists averaged $53,230 annually in 2015. However, makeup artists who work on big-budget films or with high-profile actors can earn more than $115,000 annually, while those who work in cities with small media markets can expect to earn less.

Opportunities for Advancement

Many makeup artists begin their careers as assistants and advance to become full-fledged artists. Those who have experience can move up to the position of chief makeup artist, also known as makeup designer. Some individual makeup artists develop good relationships with actors who appreciate their work. These makeup artists are often requested by name when the actor begins a new project.

What Is the Future Outlook for Makeup Artists?

The BLS does not have a specific category for makeup artists but says that work for cosmetologists, hairstylists, and other estheticians is expected to grow by 10 percent through 2024.

Find Out More

Hair & Makeup Artist Network (HMAN)
121 W. Lexington Dr., Suite 332
Glendale, CA 91203
website: www.hmartistsnetwork.com

The HMAN is a professional networking organization for freelance makeup artists who work in the entertainment, fashion, salon, and bridal industries. The site offers career tools such as tips for self-promotion, advice for setting up a business, and information about financial planning. An education section contains info about hair and makeup schools and workshops and seminars.

Lipstick Angels

PO Box 480366
Los Angeles, CA 90048
website: www.lipstickangels.org

Lipstick Angels is a nonprofit organization made up of makeup artists who volunteer their time and services to uplift the spirits of hospital patients and dependent seniors. Students can volunteer to work with professionals who provide makeup services to cancer patients and other individual in need.

Make-Up Artists and Hair Stylists Guild

828 N. Hollywood Way
Burbank, CA 91505
website: www.local706.org

This is the website of union Local 706, which represents makeup artists who work in feature films, television, commercials, theatrical productions, and more. The site features photos, videos, and information about the makeup techniques used in some Hollywood's biggest productions. Students can find information about classes the guild offers in makeup, hair craft, and prosthetics.

Professional Beauty Association (PBA)

15825 N. Seventy-First St., #100
Scottsdale, AZ 85254
website: https://probeauty.org

The PBA engages in education, charitable outreach, and advocacy. The website provides business blueprints, networking opportunities, industry news, educational resources, and information about the PBA scholarship program.

Audio Engineer

What Does an Audio Engineer Do?

> ### At a Glance
> ## Audio Engineer
>
> **Minimum Educational Requirements**
> None, but an associate's or bachelor's degree is beneficial to job seekers in this highly competitive field
>
> **Personal Qualities**
> Problem solving, patience, good communication and computer skills, manual dexterity, physical strength
>
> **Certification and Licensing**
> Not mandatory, but certification from the Society of Broadcast Engineers offers an advantage
>
> **Working Conditions**
> Indoors in radio, television, movie, or recording studios; long hours are common, as is working evenings, weekends, and holidays
>
> **Salary Range**
> Median pay of $53,330 in 2015
>
> **Number of Jobs**
> About 117,200 in 2014
>
> **Future Job Outlook**
> Projected growth of 7 percent by 2024

Beyoncé is one of the most famous recording artists in the world, and millions of people know her name. The same cannot be said about DJ Swivel, a Grammy-winning audio engineer who has worked on many of Beyoncé's songs. DJ Swivel has also helped other hit makers—including Jay Z, Kanye West, and Rihanna—achieve unique sounds on their records.

While audio engineers are often unknown to the public, their work can be heard on nearly every record sold in the past century. Audio engineers are professionally trained to record, mix, and reproduce sound. They deal with the technical and mechanical aspects of recording, handling microphones, amplifiers, soundboards, computers, software, and other recording equipment.

Audio engineers are not record producers. Producers focus on the artistic and creative aspects of recording, while engineers operate soundboards (also

Audio engineers record, mix, and reproduce sound. They must be skilled in the use of microphones, amplifiers, soundboards, computers, software, and other recording equipment.

called mixing consoles) and other equipment. Audio engineer Phil Ek, who has worked with the Shins and Modest Mouse, explains his job as "the bread and butter/nuts and bolts recording of the project."

Audio engineers work in nearly every sector of the entertainment industry. Those who work with musicians are often called recording engineers. They are responsible for setting up a singer's microphone, placing numerous mics around a drum kit, and plugging guitars, keyboards, and other electronic instruments into the soundboard. Recording engineers often consult with artists days or weeks before a recording session. Before a session, engineers set up all the equipment in a studio and work with musicians to achieve good instrumental and vocal sounds. During a recording session, engineers take on various roles. Some only turn the knobs on soundboards to control the tone and volume of each performer. Others take part in the creative process, advising musicians on ways to generate new sounds.

Audio engineers often work with professionals called mix engineers. Mix engineers play an important role in recording because most songs consist of numerous tracks, or performances, that are recorded at different times. On a rock song, for example, the bass, drum, and rhythm guitar tracks might be recorded first. Lead guitar players and vocalists will then record their performances separately, often with numerous different takes. Mix engineers use computers and other equipment to seamlessly mix together the various tracks into a final track known as a mixdown.

Miles Walker is a Grammy Award–winning mix engineer who has worked with Usher and Katy Perry. In a 2015 interview on the Your EDM website, Walker explained that a lot of his job involves bringing the artist's vision to life. "A mixing engineer . . . will take the individual sounds and blend them together so you can hear everything clear and as it was imagined in the mind of the artist," he said. "They can also do things like add special effects that complement the song, highlighting special moments, or creating ambient moods that go along with the sentiment of the song or production."

Live sound engineers typically work at concert venues such as nightclubs and arenas. They might also work in hotels, schools, government buildings, and private homes. Live sound engineers set up sound systems, speakers, monitors, amplifiers, and microphones or supervise crews that perform these jobs. The engineers conduct sound checks before a gig and adjust sound levels on mixing consoles in front of the stage during a performance.

Broadcast engineers are those who work in television and radio. They set up, maintain, and operate sound equipment, computers, and transmitters used in broadcasting. These engineers also set up equipment for remote broadcasts—that is, broadcasting done from live news events at locations outside the studio.

Finally, professionals called sound engineer technicians work on television and movie sets, where they record the audio performance of actors. Their work involves synchronizing vocal tracks with video recordings.

How Do You Become an Audio Engineer?

Education

There are no specific educational requirements for those who wish to work as audio engineers. Many audio engineers are musicians who developed their technical recording skills through years of trial and error. However, sound engineering is a highly competitive field, and employers favor engineers who hold two-year associate's degrees or four-year bachelor's degrees. Students pursuing an associate's degree in sound engineering learn the fundamentals of acoustics, digital recording, music theory, audio mixing, sound reinforcement, studio maintenance, consoles, and more. With an associate's degree, an engineer can find entry-level work as an audio technician, audio installer, or sound mixer.

Those who have an associate's degree can move on to obtain a bachelor's degree in audio engineering. Bachelor's programs focus on live sound production, electronics, computer programming, digital signal processing, and editing. Students in these programs split their time between the classroom and the studio. Graduates can pursue a career as a studio manager, music producer, live sound engineer, or mix engineer.

Like other modern tech workers, audio engineers must continue to update their education and skills throughout their career. They must learn about new hardware and recording techniques, understand new industry standards and codes, and update their safety and emergency procedures.

Certification and Licensing

Audio engineers are not required to obtain certification or licenses, but those who do will have an advantage when seeking employment. There are two main sources of certification. The Society of Broadcast Engineers offers eight types of broadcasting engineering certification, two types of operator certification, and two types of broadcast network certification to audio engineers who pass an exam. Certifications include Certified Professional Broadcast Engineer, Certified

Audio Engineer, Certified Radio Operator, and Digital Radio Broadcast Specialist.

InfoComm International offers three types of audiovisual credentials: Certified Technology Specialist, AV Systems Design Specialist, and AV System Installation Specialist.

Volunteer Work and Internships

Some audio engineers begin their careers as volunteers, working as studio assistants and "gofers" who do everything from pour coffee to wrap up wires and put away equipment after a recording session. Major studios also hire interns; this is a good way to pick up valuable work skills. DJ Swivel started as an intern; he graduated from a sound engineering program at Full Sail University in 2005, moved to New York City two days later, and was soon offered an internship at the famed Jungle City Studios. Swivel described his internship to *Billboard* magazine in 2011: "I was cleaning toilets, ordering food, doing maintenance around the studio when I first started. But it never felt like a day of work. That's when I knew I'd found my calling." Within a year, Swivel was working as an audio engineer for the hip-hop star Fabolous.

Mentorships are another way for audio engineers to improve their skills. The Society of Broadcast Engineers hosts a mentor program for those who are new to the field. Seasoned professionals partner with new engineers with fewer than five years' experience. The program involves face-to-face or telephone meetings every two weeks.

Skills and Personality

Audio engineers need good listening and communication skills. They have to follow detailed technical instructions from producers, musicians, and directors. They also need to make sure equipment is properly set up before broadcasts, performances, and recording sessions. Sound crews depend on audio engineers to give clear, concise orders.

As with any tech job, good computer skills are a must. Modern recording equipment is completely digital. Therefore, audio engineers spend their days working with computers, laptops, and tablets running recording and broadcasting apps.

Audio engineers need good manual dexterity and physical strength. Sorting and plugging in dozens of wires and cables requires a good eye and a steady hand. Audio engineers also deal with small dials, knobs, and sliders. Strong muscles and proper lifting techniques are also required to move heavy consoles, speakers, drums, and amplifiers.

Audio engineers are also problem solvers who need to be organized and mentally prepared to deal with malfunctions, equipment breakdowns, and any of the other problems that can arise in a studio filled with dozens of pieces of sensitive equipment.

On the Job

Employers

A student who completes a degree program will have a portfolio called a sound design demo reel. This consists of tracks that he or she personally engineered in the studio. A prospective engineer without a degree should also create a sound design demo reel. Demo reels should feature an audio engineer's best work. The reel should also be short, under four minutes. Employers who sift through dozens of applicant demo reels do not want or need a twelve-minute symphony of sound. A demo reel should be uploaded to either a personal website or a file-sharing site like SoundCloud, where it can be accessed by record producers, musicians and employers at recording studios, production companies, and local television and radio stations.

Working Conditions

Audio engineers who work in broadcasting generally work forty hours a week. However, the job often entails working nights, weekends, and holidays. Those who work in the recording industry can expect to work musician hours; they might enter the studio in the late afternoon and not leave until the sun rises the following morning. For example, when DJ Swivel worked with Beyoncé in 2010, he was in the studio 120 hours a week—every waking hour. As he joked in 2011: "I spent more time with Beyoncé in the last year than I have with my own family in six years."

During those long studio hours, engineers find themselves with a lot of downtime. They must wait patiently as musicians rehearse the next song, listen to music they already recorded, and—oftentimes—argue over the way the song is developing. Working in a studio can also be bad for a person's health; recording engineers are exposed to loud sounds that can permanently damage their hearing, and many musicians smoke while recording.

Earnings

According to the Bureau of Labor Statistics (BLS), the median annual wage for audio engineers was $53,330 in 2015. Those who work as broadcast engineers earn less, $37,490 per year. In the middle range, audiovisual techs make about $41,440 annually. Audio engineers who work with superstars earn considerably more. DJ Swivel is a millionaire thanks to his work with Beyoncé and others.

What Is the Future Outlook for Audio Engineers?

The BLS says employment for sound engineers is expected to grow by 7 percent through 2024. The outlook for audiovisual techs is expected to grow faster, by 12 percent by 2024.

Find Out More

Audio Engineering Society (AES)
551 Fifth Ave., #1225
New York, NY 10176
website: www.aes.org

The AES is a nonprofit organization devoted to professionals in the audio technology industry. The AES accepts student members, who can enter recording competitions, publish blogs, and find information about educational and career opportunities.

InfoComm International
11242 Waples Mill Rd., Suite 200
Fairfax, VA 22030
website: www.infocomm.org

InfoComm International is a trade association for the professional audiovisual and information communications industry. The association offers three types of certification for audio engineers. InfoComm University provides online courses, conducts webinars, and offers training at local events. Its website offers job listings, career advice, and other employment tools.

Society of Broadcast Engineers (SBE)
9102 N. Meridian St., Suite 150
Indianapolis, IN 46260
website: www.sbe.org

The SBE is a professional organization of television and radio engineers and those in related fields. The organization provides certification in various audio engineering fields, and SBE University offers online courses and webinars, mentor programs, scholarships, and career advice.

Society of Professional Audio Recording Services (SPARS)
website: www.spars.com

SPARS was founded in 1979 to advance education in the recording business for professionals and students. The organization has a mentoring program and an awards program, and it offers career advice to members.

Concert Promoter

What Does a Concert Promoter Do?

In 1997 Paul Tollett was a struggling thirty-one-year-old concert promoter whose company, Goldenvoice, was failing. Tollett got the idea to put on a two-day music festival in the middle of the California desert. He would book musicians with a reputation for artistry rather than producing number one hits. With this, the Coachella Valley Music and Arts Festival was born. Today Coachella is a three-day event that attracts nearly two hundred thousand people and earns over $84 million a year. During the early years, fewer than fifty thousand people purchased Coachella tickets annually, and Tollett's company lost millions of investor dollars. In a 2009 interview with *LA Weekly*, Tollett explained the contradictory nature of his profession. "We were scared to death [losing all that money], I'll admit that," he said. "But in real time, when you're a promoter, your job is to promote. You're supposed to be exuberant. You're supposed to say that every band is the greatest. We have the best lineup in the world. That's your job, to get the word out."

At a Glance

Concert Promoter

Minimum Educational Requirements

None

Personal Qualities

Good communication and business skills, ability to focus in stressful situations, patience, good negotiation skills

Working Conditions

Indoors in offices during the day, nights and weekends at concert venues

Salary Range

From $40,000 to $114,000 a year in 2015

Number of Jobs

About 53,190 in 2016

Future Job Outlook

Projected growth of 13 percent through 2020

As Tollett makes clear, concert promoters must perform their job with a smile no matter what their mood. According to the website Careers in Music, concert promoters perform sixty to eighty different tasks for each show, each as important as the next. Their number one task is to find a musical act or group of acts that will draw a large enough crowd to make for a successful show. This requires the ability to recognize talent and understand what the public wants. As entertainment journalist Rachel Grate explained in 2016 on the Eventbrite website, "As a concert promoter, you make a living by knowing the next big artist before they're big."

When deciding to promote a concert, a promoter will make a financial offer to an artist and sign a contract to cement the deal. This involves working through talent buyers, booking agents, and personal managers who have connections to the act. The promoter then books an appropriate venue, choosing a club or concert hall that will not be too large or too small for the expected crowd. With the talent and venue in place, the promoter creates marketing and advertising plans and works with artists to create posters, fliers, and ads that run in newspapers and magazines. Concerts are promoted on social media sites, and if the act is big enough, a promoter buys billboard space and ads on TV and radio.

Weeks before the concert takes place, promoters book air and ground transportation and hotel rooms for the artists and staff. They hire vendors, including security personnel, caterers, and even massage therapists and other health care personnel to work with the talent. Promoters ensure the stage is constructed and the sound and lighting systems are ready and reliable before the show. On the day of the show, the promoter oversees the load in, which is when stage, sound, and lighting equipment is brought into the venue and assembled. When the show is over, the promoter makes sure the load out goes smoothly.

Promoters have to deal with government officials to get concert permits; they also work with insurance companies to provide policies that cover accidents and other liabilities. Promoters also deal with union officials, who oversee rules concerning schedules, tasks, and pay for stagehands, truck drivers, electricians, and other union workers.

Concert promotion has a lot of moving parts, and many things can go wrong. Performances can be delayed or canceled if an artist misses a flight or other travel connections. A newspaper might mistakenly print the wrong date or time in an advertisement. Sound or light equipment can fail in the middle of a show. And every promoter lies awake at night worrying if enough people will attend a show to make the effort worthwhile.

How to Become a Concert Promoter

Education

While concert promoters do not necessarily need to go to college, an academic education can lead to success. Promoters deal with contracts, legal issues, advertising, large sums of money, and huge numbers of people. Anyone with advanced math, business, and communication skills therefore has an advantage in this field. As concert promoter Robbie Kowal explains on Careers in Music, writing skills can be very useful. He offers the following advice to prospective concert promoters:

> Learn how to write. I don't mean 140 characters and I don't mean a blog post. Learn how to write a press release and effectively communicate in long form. . . . Learning how to write teaches you how to organize your thoughts and effectively communicate a point and in the case of a show, your point is why you should spend money to go see this band.

Concert promoters also need to have good computer skills. Most promoters use accounting programs like Excel and QuickBooks to pay bills, generate invoices, and keep track of expenses. Promoters need to be able to read and understand the spreadsheets generated by the programs. Familiarity with graphic design applications like Photoshop and Illustrator comes in handy when a promoter needs to make or resize fliers, posters, and other artwork. Promoters also need to understand the very dense and technical language used in contracts.

Many of the skills needed to promote concerts are learned through trial and error on the job. Promoters learn to be cautious, trust their instincts, and have the confidence to pass on deals that might not be profitable.

Volunteer Work and Internships

The best way to become an independent promoter is to "intern with a small company or small club and learn how the real world works," says Kowal. "Then throw a party, see what works. Do a small party so if you lose all that money you'll be ok. [Do it] just to see if you like it."

Prospective concert promoters should also attend all types of concerts, not just those put on by acts they enjoy. When attending a concert, they will get a chance to observe and dissect the numerous shifting facets of the scene. They can watch what happens before, during, and after shows. Prospective concert promoters often stand off to the side of the stage, watch set changes between acts, and observe the stagehands and sound techs as they switch out microphones, tune guitars, and set up amplifiers and drums. They also check out security, make a note of fences and perimeters, and watch ticket takers, door guards, and anyone driving around in golf carts. They take note of bartenders and food and merchandise vendors, watching how they operate, how many people they serve, and how money is handled.

Skills and Personality

Concert promotion is based on getting the word out and advertising to as many potential attendees as possible. That means it is critical to have good communication skills. Promoters must also be very efficient and be able to deal with the demands of work crews, petulant artists, rude managers, nonstop phone calls, and numerous simultaneous emergencies. They must also cope with the stress of not knowing whether a show will sell out or flop. As concert promoter Rob Warwick says in an interview with Rock.It Boy Entertainment, "You need nerves of steel, you have to be able to react quickly to change, you have to be able to be aggressive when needed and finally, you have to be a skilled negotiator."

On the Job

Employers

There are several ways a person can work as a concert promoter. Some specialize as talent buyers for bars and clubs. These people work "in house"—for a single small venue—where they book and promote acts for a percentage of the ticket sales.

In-house promoters often do independent, or indie, concert promotion on the side. Indie promoters depend on ticket sales to pay their bills and salary. They secure venues, book talent, and carry out the other tasks necessary to promote a concert. As music industry blogger TJ Bear explained in 2015 on the Music Industry How To website: "[Indie] promoters assume the most risk. Although just about anyone can do it this usually takes a heavy financial investment, a solid understanding of the business and industry, and good relationships with music venues and booking agents."

Indie promoters must compete with the two industry giants: Live Nation and AEG Live, which earned a combined $3 billion in 2015. These two companies controlled an estimated 70 percent of all live music production in the United States. Those who want a steady paycheck and benefits can work as promoters for these concert behemoths. The right job can provide great experience for those who wish to strike out on their own in the future.

Working Conditions

Concert promoters will work long hours while a project is unfolding. They spend their days in the office making phone calls, sending e-mails and texts, and holding meetings with artists, managers, vendors, and other stakeholders. Evenings and weekends are spent attending concerts—either their own productions or those put on by others, where they can learn and network. The business is highly competitive, and rivals can be a big problem. "Some promoters really play nasty with each other and actively try to put each other out of business," says Kowal.

Earnings

Concert promotion is a turbulent business, and there is no guarantee indie promoters will get a regular paycheck. Promoters just starting out barely break even—if they are lucky. Others lose considerable amounts of money. However, indie promoters who succeed can expect to make anywhere from $40,000 to $114,000 annually, according to the Bureau of Labor Statistics (BLS). Like with many other jobs in the entertainment business, those who succeed can succeed big time: The Berklee College of Music found that indie promoters can earn up to $1 million a year if they book large venues, popular music acts, and numerous shows.

Opportunities for Advancement

Concert promoters are traditionally self-employed. Many begin their careers working in clubs as disc jockeys, bartenders, or sound engineers. They befriend artists, road managers, and others involved in the concert business. They build relationships over time that allow them to move into concert promotion. For example, Rob Warwick began his career doing security, which allowed him to meet bands and network with booking agents. "This business is all about relationships and networking," says Warwick. "When I first started, I had to get in front of agents and start building solid relationships. I was actively knocking on doors, going to agencies and selling myself. . . . Eventually, I built up trust and the agents began to call me."

What Is the Future Outlook for Concert Promoters?

The BLS categorizes concert promoters as "Promoters of Performing Arts, Sports, and Similar Events." This job category is expected to grow by 13 percent through 2020. The growth can be traced to a growing interest in music festivals and other live music events.

Find Out More

International Entertainment Buyers Association (IEBA)
412 E. Iris Dr.
Nashville, TN 37204
website: www.ieba.org

The IEBA is a nonprofit organization for live entertainment industry professionals. The organization awards several types of scholarships and sponsors summer internships for prospective concert promoters and others.

International Festivals & Events Association (IFEA)
2603 W. Eastover Terrace
Boise, ID 83706
website: www.ifea.com

This association caters to professionals who create festivals and other public events. The IFEA provides educational webinars, a career network, professional education opportunities, and other resources of interest to future concert promoters.

Pollstar
4697 W. Jacquelyn Ave.
Fresno, CA 93722
website: www.pollstar.com

This trade publication for the concert tour industry provides insight into the work performed by agents, managers, and promoters. The organization publishes a weekly magazine and six directories, which include concert industry contact data, artist tour histories, and other information useful to anyone wishing to become a concert promoter.

Film or TV Director

What Does a Film or TV Director Do?

Film directors such as Steven Spielberg, James Cameron, George Lucas, and Kathryn Bigelow are among the most famous people in the entertainment business. Their films have generated billions of dollars and have been viewed by countless people throughout the world. Bigelow, who directed Academy Award–winning films like *The Hurt Locker* and *Zero Dark Thirty*, described the impact a director can have on society in the 2007 book *Women Directors and Their Films*: "I recognized film as this extraordinary social tool that could reach tremendous numbers of people."

Film directors strive to tell memorable stories while supervising all of a movie's dramatic, artistic, and technical components. They oversee the three main phases of filming: preproduction, production, and postproduction. The preproduction process begins when a director teams up with a producer. The producer's job is to raise money, hire key personnel, secure shooting locations, and arrange for distribution. Producers create a film budget and shooting

At a Glance
Film or TV Director

Minimum Educational Requirements
None

Personal Qualities
Creative, decisive, ambitious, patient; must have strong leadership, motivational, communication, and technical skills

Working Conditions
Indoors in offices and studios, outdoors on location

Salary Range
Median pay of $68,400 in 2015

Number of Jobs
About 122,600 in 2014

Future Job Outlook
Projected growth of 9 percent by 2024

schedule, which directors are required to follow as closely as possible.

Script development is an important aspect of preproduction. This requires the director to consult with authors and screenwriters to either create a new story or write a script—called a screenplay—from an existing book, play, or tale. During preproduction, directors also work with professionals called casting directors; it is their job to assign actors, singers, and dancers to specific roles in the production. Before shooting begins, directors also scout for locations to film each scene. They also work with makeup artists and costume designers to create drawings and mockups of various looks, hairstyles, and outfits for actors.

The second phase, production, is the toughest part of directing. Most films are shot in two to three weeks, with everyone working fourteen to eighteen hours a day. During this time, a director coordinates the actions of lighting, sound, and camera crews. The director's main job is to inspire actors to achieve their best performances. This often involves explaining the motivations and background of a character to help the actor better understand the role.

Directors also tell actors where to stand, how to move through a scene, which emotions to display, and how to say their lines for best effect. Film director Elliot Grove describes the production process on the Raindance website: "Everything happens at once. The actors, lights, camera, props, schedule, film stock, egos, temper tantrums, and all the rest. Production, although typically presented as being fun and joyous, will probably be the worst two or three weeks of your life. But you persevere."

After a shoot is over, the director will have about twenty hours of rough footage that consists of multiple takes of each scene. During postproduction, the director works closely with an editor to cut the scenes together into a coherent film. Postproduction also finds the director working with a soundtrack composer and a person called a Foley artist, who creates sound effects such as footsteps, car motors, and explosions.

The work of a television director is different from that of a movie director, and the jobs are viewed differently in the entertainment industry. Movies are considered a director's medium. This means that directors have all the creative control. Television is not a director's medium but a writer's medium; a TV series is managed by the head writer, who is called a showrunner. The showrunner supervises a number of directors, each assigned to shoot specific episodes of a program. The tasks of TV showrunners are similar to those of movie directors; they develop story lines, hire and fire crew members, cast actors, follow budgets, and have final say over every shot. This limits the director's creative input.

A TV director's job is limited to supervising placement of cameras, lights, and other equipment and mapping out the movements and actions of actors. Actors on TV shows usually have well-established roles and need little in the way of direction in terms of their character's motivations and emotions. Nicole Holofcener has directed both films and TV shows. On the Vulture website, she describes the difference between the two mediums: "[On my own set], if I feel I've gotten a good take and the scene is done, I say, 'Cut!' and we move on. But if I'm [directing] a television show, I turn to the writer probably about 5,000 times a day to say, 'Did we get it? Are you happy? Do you want me to try anything else?'"

How Do You Become a Film or TV Director?

Education

There are no specific educational requirements for film or TV directors. But there are numerous steps a person can take to break into this extremely competitive field. The first step is easy—watch as many classic movies as possible, especially those made by history's great directors such as Steven Spielberg, James Cameron, Alfred Hitchcock, Martin Scorsese, Orson Wells, Stanley Kubrick, and others. Most of the classics can be seen on cable TV, checked out of a library, or streamed. One helpful trick is to watch the films with the sound off, as independent director Gabe Moura explains on the Elements of Cinema website: "This is the perfect technique if you want to observe how stories are told visually, and how the camera behaves to provoke this or that. . . . This film-viewing approach will make you aware of every camera setup, including angles, shot sizes, and movements."

Moura also recommends reading as many screenplays as possible. Websites like Daily Script and IMSDb contain hundreds of scripts from popular movies, which viewers can read while watching the film. This exercise is helpful in two ways: It shows how a film is created from words on a page , and provides students with an additional means for learning how to write scripts. Moura explains why this skill is important:

> No one is going to give you a chance at directing right away, you have to earn it. One way to prove yourself and build the confidence of investors is to write screenplays. Film directing is storytelling, and you have to prove that you have the principles of storytelling down so that producers can bet on you. So my suggestion is write screenplays as often as you can and make sure they're good. . . . It is much easier for a screenwriter to become a director than for a nobody to become a director.

Prospective directors should also take acting classes and learn various acting methods. This is a great way to learn how actors speak, think, and perform—skills that are central to a director's job.

The most important thing a prospective director can do is to assemble a director's reel—a portfolio of original work. A director's reel features a number of short films that have dialogue, sound effects, and music. Directors are hired on the strength of their reel, which might consist of a few TV commercials or a montage of beautiful shots.

Every director needs a reel, but James Cameron believes that almost anyone can make one. Cameron offered this expert advice in a 2006 interview posted on YouTube: "Pick up a camera. Shoot something. No matter how small, no matter how cheesy, no matter whether your friends and your sister star in it. Put your name on it as director. Now you're a director. Everything after that you're just negotiating your budget and your fee."

There are numerous film schools and colleges that prospective directors can attend. Schools offer courses in shooting, acting, scriptwriting, and technical aspects of moviemaking, such as lighting, sound, and camera work. But whether film school is helpful is a subject of much debate. Film school is very expensive, and many world-famous directors, including Quentin Tarantino, Steven Spielberg, Ridley Scott, and Peter Jackson, actually did not attend one. All have made statements that support Cameron's advice—pick up a camera and start shooting. However, film school gives students access to equipment, professional advice, networks, and internship positions that often prove useful in the future.

Volunteer Work and Internships

Film studios offer internships in various positions, including creative development, finance, and digital media. Most studio internships require interns to have a degree from a film school. Production interns help directors film movies. People who land these internships can move into jobs as assistant directors, directors of photography, and other positions.

Skills and Personality

A director's primary job is to tell a great story. This is accomplished by managing actors, large crews, highly technical equipment, and numerous theatrical elements like props and costumes. The film also needs to resonate with the public—at least, enough of the public to make a profit for the studio and those who invested in the movie. The job requires a set of skills not often found in a single person. For example, directors must be creative visionaries but also exude a strong sense of authority. They need to communicate their artistic vision decisively to inspire actors and technicians to produce the best work possible, often under difficult circumstances. Directors need a tremendous sense of drive and ambition but must also exhibit grace under pressure. Directors must also be problem solvers open to improvising when things do not go as planned.

On the Job

Employers

Directors often begin their careers as independent filmmakers or by directing music videos or television commercials. Directors of TV shows might start out working on local talk shows and news programs. Those who have a good director's reel can seek employment with producers who do the hiring for major films. Producers are always looking for new talent but also know that experienced directors can bring a project in on budget and on time. While most aspiring directors do not get handed multimillion-dollar blockbusters, some first-time directors do get that opportunity. For example, Rupert Sanders was hired to direct *Snow White and the Huntsman* after producing nothing more than a short film called *Black Hole*.

Working Conditions

Film and TV directors work indoors at studios on the set of a movie film or a TV show or work outdoors on location. The work can be stressful, and directors often work long hours on nights and weekends. They might need to travel locally, across the country, or overseas.

Earnings

Many professional film directors work under guidelines developed by the Directors Guild of America (DGA). Pay is based on the type of production. For example, film classifications include shorts, documentaries, low budget, and high budget. Each pays a different scale. Directors who work a high-budget film (over $11 million) earned a minimum of $16,508 a week in 2014. Short and documentary film directors earned $2,948 a day. Top film directors earn a percentage of ticket sales, which nets them even higher earnings. However, many filmmakers work only a few days or weeks per year. This lowers the average annual wage calculated by the Bureau of Labor Statistics (BLS), which says that the median income for directors in 2015 was $68,400.

Opportunities for Advancement

Some directors begin their careers as assistant directors. The first assistant director determines the shooting order of scenes, draws up shooting schedules, and coordinates various activities on the orders of the director. The second assistant director works as a backstage manager; he or she collaborates with actors and puts the cast through makeup and wardrobe. These positions offer assistants opportunities to advance to the position of director. Other directors begin as commercial and music video directors before moving on to the big screen.

What Is the Future Outlook for Film or TV Directors?

Job growth in the film, television, and video industry is expected to grow in the coming years as streaming services like Amazon, Hulu, and Netflix produce more original programming. For this reason, the BLS expect the number of director jobs to grow by 9 percent by 2024.

Find Out More

Academy of Television Arts & Sciences

5220 Lankershim Blvd.
North Hollywood, CA 91601
website: www.emmys.org

This organization hands out Emmy Awards in dozens of technical, creative, and craft categories. It also provides intern opportunities and college television awards. The academy's Mister Rogers Memorial Scholarship Program awards scholarships to college students.

Daily Script

website: www.dailyscript.com

This website has hundreds of scripts from famous films that prospective directors can read to familiarize themselves with the director's most basic task—translating words on paper to images on-screen.

Directors Guild of America (DGA)

7920 Sunset Blvd.
Los Angeles, CA 90046
website: www.dga.com

The DGA represents the interests of around sixteen thousand directors, assistant directors, and other professionals. The guild produces informative podcasts and holds numerous award ceremonies, including the DGA Student Film Awards.

Warner Bros. Careers: Internships

website: www.warnerbroscareers.com

Summer internships at Warner Bros. are for students currently enrolled in an accredited undergraduate or graduate program. Interns assist screen-writers, production assistants, technical personnel, and others who provide skills useful to a prospective director.

Interview with a Musician

Camile Baudoin is a full-time professional musician in New Orleans, Louisiana. He has played lead guitar with the jam band the Radiators since 1978, performs annually at the New Orleans Jazz & Heritage Festival, and was inducted into the Louisiana Music Hall of Fame in 2011.

Q: Why did you decide to become a musician?

A: I grew up with music around me. My dad played guitar a little bit and when I was ten years old he bought a guitar and he taught me what he knew how to play on it. I seemed to have a knack for playing the guitar. Music got me out of myself and helped me to socialize and interact with people. From the beginning I saw that playing music brought much joy to people's lives.

Q: Can you describe your typical workday (or night)?

A: Each musician is responsible for getting themselves and their equipment to the venue. After all the musicians have arrived and have set up their gear, a sound check is usually in order. You have a great night playing your music. When you are finished, you may take a short break and come back out to sign autographs and just hang with the fans for a bit. You may have to pack up your gear at some point—if you don't have someone to do that for you.

Q: What do you like most about your job?

A: The most rewarding thing about playing music is making a positive difference in people's lives. I was lucky to have so much fun making a decent living for decades. I'm still playing and having a blast. I truly believe music is keeping me young at heart and in good health. I still meet wonderful folks all the time.

Q: What do you like least about your job?
A: The traveling gets tiresome and wears you out after years of doing it.

Q: What personal qualities do you find most valuable for this type of work?
A: Dedication, patience, tenacity, passion, and love of people and life. Also, a sense of humor!

Q: What are the business aspects of working as a professional musician?
A: The "business" of music is in flux and will probably be for a while. If you are a band leader, you will supervise the gigs, recordings, promo, gear/equipment, and personnel. You will sometimes find yourself in the role of friend, mom, dad, psychiatrist, roadie, navigator, etc. I say this not to scare or dismay you, but to point out the various things that may be part of what you may encounter as a working musician. For me, it's all worth it. I grumble sometimes, but most jobs have mundane parts to them.

Q: What advice would you give to musicians just starting out as far as booking gigs?
A: First, have your music and your band together and rehearsed. When an opportunity presents itself, you want to be ready. Whatever energy and input you provide, luck may play a large role in what happens in a music career. That being said, tenacity doesn't hurt. DO NOT sign any long-term commitments before you learn the ropes. It is a learning curve. The great part of this is that you get to play your music while doing the "work."

Q: What do you suggest musicians do to promote their music?
A: Talk to anyone who will give you their ear. Learn what's happening and go to music seminars in your area. Talk to musicians you may know. Hire someone to do promo as things progress.

Q: What changes do you see on the horizon for live music?

A: Some promoters have recently been doing what I call cluster billing; there are several acts on a bill of different genres to help promote ticket sales. As of late I've seen a lot of specialty, intimate shows at people's houses where the gathering is smaller, but the fans get an intimate music performance.

Q: What are your current musical projects?

A: Playing with several different bands and various musicians. Putting together my next music CD download. Learning new ways of playing old things. Practicing awkward fingerings and always learning new licks with passion!

Q: What advice do you have for students who might be interested in a career as a musician?

A: I would suggest going to music school where you can learn from many different sources, learn music theory and how to read music, and learn the music business. I took music courses through two years of college. I also went to the school of the streets. I went to see many musicians play and tried to learn from them. Many of the older musicians were very kind with their time and taught me a lot.

Other Jobs in Entertainment

Agent
Animator
Art director
Casting director
Choreographer
Church choir director
Commercial jingle composer
Costume designer
Cruise ship performer
Dancer
Ensemble director
Entertainment attorney
Film composer
Film editor
Foley artist
Front of house engineer
FX editor
Gaffer
Grip
Instrument builder
Instrument sales
Licensing administrator
Location manager
Location sound engineer
Lyricist/songwriter
Music arranger
Music curator
Music journalist
Music teacher
Music therapist
Piano tuner
Production designer
Publicist
Set dresser
Social media strategist
Stage manager
Theater director
Tour director
Video game composer

Editor's note: The US Department of Labor's Bureau of Labor Statistic provides information about hundreds of occupations. The agency's *Occupational Outlook Handbook* describes what these jobs entail, the work environment, education and skill requirements, pay, future outlook, and more. The *Occupational Outlook Handbook* may be accessed online at www.bls.gov/ooh.

Index

Picture Credits

6: Maury Aaseng

11: iStockphoto/People Images

33: iStockphoto/Warren Goldswain

41: Thinkstock Images/Eyecandy Images

49: Thinkstock Images/iStock

About the Author

Stuart A. Kallen is the author of more than 350 nonfiction books for children and young adults. He has written on topics ranging from the theory of relativity to the art of electronic dance music. In addition, Kallen has written award-winning children's videos and television scripts. In his spare time he is a singer, songwriter, and guitarist in San Diego.